ANDERSON S0-AXP-514

Contemporary Hispanic Americans

GLORIA ESTEFAN

BY
JANEL RODRIGUEZ

RSVP
RAINTREE
STECK-VAUGHN
PUBLISHERS
The Steck-Vaughn Company

Austin, Texas

Copyright © **1996, Steck-Vaughn Company.** All rights reserved. No part of this book may be reproduced or utilized in any form or by any means, electronic or mechanical, including photocopying, recording, or by any information storage and retrieval system, without permission in writing from the copyright owner. Requests for permission to make copies of any part of the work should be mailed to: Copyright Permissions, Steck-Vaughn Company, P.O. Box 26015, Austin, Texas 78755

Published by Raintree Steck-Vaughn, an imprint of Steck-Vaughn Company.
Produced by Mega-Books, Inc.
Design and Art Direction by Michaelis/Carpelis Design Associates.
Cover photo: Ken Nahoum

Library of Congress Cataloging-in-Publication Data
Rodriguez, Janel.
    Gloria Estefan / Janel Rodriguez
        p.   cm. — (Contemporary Hispanic Americans)
    Includes index.
    Summary: Examines the life of the Cuban born pop star who sings, dances, composes, and records with the Miami Sound Machine.
    ISBN 0-8172-3982-0 (Hardcover)
    ISBN 0-8114-9788-7 (Softcover)
    1. Estefan, Gloria—Juvenile literature. 2. Singers—United States—Biography—Juvenile Literature. [1. Estefan, Gloria. 2. Singers. 3. Rock music. 4. Cuban Americans—Biography. 5. Women—Biography.]   I. Title. II. Series.
ML3930.E85R6   1996
782.42164 '092—dc20   95-16152
[B]   CIP
                                                                           AC
Printed and bound in the United States.

1 2 3 4 5 6 7 8 9 LB 99 98 97 96 95

Photo credits: Haviland/Star File: p.4; Todd Kaplan/Star File: pp. 19, 25; AP/Wide World Photos Inc.: pp. 29, 30; UPI/Bettmann: pp. 11, 13, 35, 37; Mark Hinojosa/*New York Newsday*: p. 33; Reuters/Bettmann: p. 41; Malter/Retna Ltd.: p. 7; Freek Ariens/Retna Ltd.: p. 8; Susan Watts/Retna Ltd.: p. 15; Scott Weiner/Retna Ltd.: p. 17; Gregory Richard Kearney/Gamma Liaison: p. 21; Gary Gershoff/Retna Ltd.: pp. 23, 38; George Bodnar/Retna Ltd.: p. 27; A. Vico/Contifoto/Sygma: p. 43; Kathy Banks/Sygma: p.45.

Contents

One

OYE MI CANTO (HEAR MY VOICE)

I t was a cold, frosty day in March 1990. World-famous pop singer and songwriter Gloria Estefan (es-**TAY**-fahn) lay down on the couch of her tour bus and closed her eyes. She was very tired. The day before, she had been to the White House. There, President George Bush had honored her for her work to prevent drug abuse. Now Gloria was on her way to upstate New York to give a concert.

The Pennsylvania highway was slippery with snow. Gloria had just woken up when she heard a crash. Her bus lurched forward, and she was knocked to the floor. A truck had smashed into the bus from behind. Then the bus had rammed into another truck in front of it.

Gloria felt a sharp, stabbing pain in her back. She could not move. Her husband, Emilio, and their nine-

Gloria Estefan's high-energy performances have helped to make her a superstar.

year-old son, Nayib, were on the bus with her. She called out to them. Were they all right? She had to know. They, too, were injured, but they were still alive and able to talk. Gloria was relieved.

Because of winter traffic, help was slow in coming. The Estefan family waited together. When rescue crews finally arrived, they were shocked. They had not known that they would find a celebrity, waiting and in pain. They also did not want to tell Gloria how bad things looked for her.

News of the accident spread across the world. Many people were worried about Gloria, Emilio, and Nayib. How seriously were they hurt? The report soon came back from the hospital. Gloria's back was broken. She might never walk again.

Fans found it difficult to imagine Gloria Estefan unable to walk. She was famous for her high-energy performances. When they heard Gloria's name, some people thought of Latin beats and a beautiful singing voice. Others thought of Gloria's songwriting talent. Still others thought of her ad campaign to help stop young people from taking drugs. Gloria's talents and dedication had captured a lot of people's attention. When Gloria was hurt in the accident, it shocked them all.

Gloria's success was based on her incredible talent, spirit, and beauty. Some people thought she would even make a good movie star. Gloria had always refused film offers. "I don't feel like an actress," she said. "I'm a singer. That's what I love to do."

Gloria loves to write and perform romantic ballads. "My business is to try and evoke emotion," she says.

Everyone could see that Gloria loved her work. She even wrote some of her own songs. Her favorite kinds of songs were **ballads**. These slow, romantic songs brought out people's feelings.

Besides ballads, Gloria and her band, called the Miami Sound Machine, were well known for their dance hits. Fans could move to the beats and rhythms of salsa, bembe, and disco all in one show. In concerts, when Gloria sang "Conga," people in the audience would leap from their seats. Then, they would form a line and do the Cuban dance down the aisles! Gloria would encourage them. She would tell them that the way to do the conga was to take "three steps one way, three steps the other way, and then you do whatever you want!" She was happiest when her audience got up and enjoyed themselves. "I give you a show, you give me a show," she once said.

Gloria's stardom has always been supported by her talented band, the Miami Sound Machine.

Upbeat songs and beautiful ballads were not the only reason why Gloria Estefan and the Miami Sound Machine were international stars. The band was **bilingual**. That means they could speak and sing in two different languages, Spanish and English. This gift helped them reach twice as many fans. As Gloria once told her fans at a concert in Miami, she loves seeing "so many different cultures, so many different people in one place having a good time." The audience cheered in agreement.

Some fans had known about the Miami Sound Machine since the band's early days, when they recorded only in Spanish. Some had discovered them later, with English-language hits like "Conga." After a while, their songs made the Top Forty, one after the other. Their videos played on MTV. Their albums went platinum and gold, which means they sold millions, and their concerts were always sold out. Gloria was the band's best-known member. In fact, the band eventually decided to call themselves by the name of their star: Gloria Estefan.

Gloria's fans knew a lot about her, but they did not know everything. They did not know what a fighter she was. One month after her accident, Gloria was still in bad shape. Yet she was determined to get well. Life had given Gloria Estefan many hardships, as well as many gifts. She had faced them all with spirit—and she was not about to stop now.

Chapter Two

EYES OF
INNOCENCE

As a girl, Gloria Estefan was chubby and shy. No one would have guessed she was going to be a pop superstar when she grew up. "When I was shy," Gloria said, "I felt I had something in me I wanted to bring out. I just didn't know how to do it."

Gloria Estefan was born Gloria Fajardo. The Fajardo family was originally from Cuba, an island south of Florida in the Caribbean Sea. Gloria was born in Havana, Cuba's capital, on September 1, 1957.

At that time, the dictator of Cuba was Fulgencio Batista y Zaldivar. He had seized power in 1952 by overthrowing the government. Fighting against him could mean death. In January 1959, however, some people decided to try. Led by Fidel Castro and Ernesto "Che" Guevara, they formed an army of their own and defeated Batista's army.

Gloria's father, José Fajardo, had been in the losing army. Fidel Castro's new government started putting

Gloria's family, like many Cuban exiles, settled in an area of Miami known as "Little Havana," shown here in 1963.

Batista's soldiers in jail. Some of Batista's supporters were even being killed. José Fajardo knew he had to get his wife and baby Gloria out of the country or their lives would be in danger. Soon after Castro's takeover, the Fajardos escaped to the United States.

The Fajardos eventually settled in Miami, Florida, along with many other Cubans. These Cubans considered themselves exiles. Exiles are people forced to live away from their homeland.

José Fajardo wanted to see Fidel Castro defeated. Then, he and his family could move back home. So, in 1961, he joined an army made up of other exiles. They tried a sneak attack on their homeland, but it failed.

Many of the exiles, including Gloria's father, were captured and held prisoner in Cuba.

Back in Miami, Gloria remembers, "All the men were gone. All the mothers and kids were living together." It was a difficult time for the Cubans in Florida. Many of them—including Gloria and her mother—still spoke only Spanish. Housing was hard to find. The Fajardos lived in a tiny apartment in an area that came to be called "Little Havana," after the Cuban capital. The Cubans also faced a lot of prejudice in Miami. Many non-Hispanic people did not welcome the exiles and treated them unfairly.

It was Gloria's mother and grandmother who taught Gloria to turn to music when things got tough. Many of the women who were missing their husbands, sons, and brothers would gather together for comfort. They would sing traditional songs of their homeland to feel better. "Little Gloria," or "Glorita," as Gloria was called, would sing with them.

In late 1962, President John F. Kennedy made a deal with Cuba. Gloria's father and the other prisoners from the failed attack were released. José Fajardo returned to his family in Miami. That year, the Fajardos had a very grateful Christmas.

However, Gloria's father had not had enough of being a soldier. José Fajardo soon joined the United States Army. He became a captain, and volunteered to fight in the Vietnam War. For Gloria and her family, it was another difficult time. Despite the stress and strain, Gloria did well in school. She learned English quickly, and it became one of her best subjects. Her favorite hobby was listening to music.

After two years of fighting in Vietnam, Gloria's father returned home once again. Soon, the family noticed a change in him. He was tired all the time, and he began to complain of pain and numbness. Soon, he could not stand without help.

José Fajardo was tested at a local hospital. There, doctors discovered that he had multiple sclerosis, also known as M.S. This disease affects the brain, muscles,

Many Cuban exiles, including Gloria's father, hoped to one day return to Cuba. Here, protesters in front of the White House ask the United States government for help in overthrowing Fidel Castro.

and nerves. Slowly, it takes away a person's ability to move. This meant that eventually Mr. Fajardo would need a wheelchair. Later, he would be so weak that he would need to stay in bed and be looked after.

The Fajardo family was shocked and saddened by the news. Because Mr. Fajardo could no longer work, Gloria's mother got a job and started going to night school. In Cuba, she had been a teacher. To be a teacher in America, she had to learn English.

Gloria, who was only eleven years old, took care of her father and her younger sister Rebecca. "Music was my escape," she says. When the burden of caring for her family became too much, Gloria would lock herself in her room and sing. Instead of crying, Gloria expressed her emotions through music. In such sad times, singing was a positive way to let go. Soon, she also learned to play the guitar.

Gloria started attending a Catholic high school called Lourdes Academy. With things so tough at home, she had to work harder to get good grades. The stress in her private life showed in everything. She became very shy and quiet. "I was handling a lot, trying to be strong for my mom," Gloria says.

With encouragement from her teachers, Gloria found the courage to perform at an assembly. The school audience applauded Gloria when she was done. That gave her even more courage. She enrolled in a music class where she met other musicians and music lovers.

Gloria began singing and playing the guitar as a way to express her own emotions. Later, the feelings expressed in her music would touch millions of fans.

When Gloria was sixteen, her father's health took a bad turn. He was too sick for his own family to care for him any longer. Mr. Fajardo went to stay in a hospital for those who had served in the military. Now, Gloria did not have to take care of her father, but she had to endure the pain of missing him.

Again, Gloria found relief in her music. She began to practice her singing with her cousin Merci. Together, the two girls often sang for their families. Gloria wanted to form a band with some girls in school, but she did not know the first thing about starting one. Luck was on Gloria's side. Just at that time, the school had invited someone to visit and give a talk on music. His name was Emilio Estefan.

Three

SOMEONE COMES INTO YOUR LIFE

When he met Gloria in 1975, Emilio Estefan was a young man with a love for music and a real drive for success. Emilio's parents were originally from Lebanon. They had moved from their Middle Eastern homeland to Cuba, where Emilio was born. Like Gloria, Emilio became interested in music as a hobby when he was young.

Life became difficult for the Estefan family under the government of Fidel Castro. The Estefans left Cuba and moved to Spain in 1966, when Emilio was thirteen. Two years later, they arrived in Miami.

Emilio's new home, like Gloria's, was poor and small. He lived with fifteen other relatives in one small apartment. Emilio knew that in a country like America he could go far with hard work. He also needed to help support his family. While he was still in school, Emilio found a job in the mailroom of a Puerto Rican–owned importing company.

Gloria and Emilio's chance meeting in 1975 was the beginning of a great musical and personal relationship that is still going strong today.

An ambitious young man, Emilio loved to play the accordion. He needed a chance to play in front of an audience. To get a start, he offered to play at a restaurant for free. The customers there liked his music very much. After that experience, Emilio knew that music would be his life.

Emilio's parents thought he was crazy. The music business was not a stable one. Most musicians were not paid very well. Besides Emilio had moved up in the importing company. He had a good, solid job. Why not stay there? Emilio promised his parents that he would not quit his job. He just wanted to become more involved in music. Surprisingly, his own boss was on his side. He hired Emilio to play at a party he was giving.

Excited about this opportunity, Emilio quickly formed a band with two other men. They played Cuban music at parties, weddings, and other occasions. They became popular around Miami, especially with Hispanic-American audiences. Eventually, Emilio got more musicians to join the band. They called themselves "The Miami Latin Boys."

Meanwhile, Gloria's hard work at school was also paying off. She received a partial scholarship to Miami University. Gloria wanted to study psychology, to learn what makes people think and feel. She was also interested in communications. With these skills, Gloria could help people learn to understand themselves and one another.

Music was another form of communication Gloria always found the time for. Music is sometimes called "the universal language." That is because it speaks to people's hearts in a way everyone can understand. Gloria knew that she wanted to continue singing. Getting a band together seemed the perfect way to make that happen.

It was Emilio who gave Gloria advice. After his talk at Lourdes Academy, he even listened to Gloria sing. He left without saying much to Gloria, but he would remember her beautiful voice. They didn't know it yet, but their meeting was an important beginning.

A few months after Emilio met Gloria, the Miami Latin Boys were performing at a wedding. Gloria and her family were guests. The band played mostly instrumental music, with very little singing. Emilio saw Gloria there and asked her to sing with the band. She was too shy to say yes right away. Finally, with her mother urging her on, Gloria accepted. After she sang, everyone stood up to applaud her! Emilio knew that Gloria was just what his band needed to be even better. Now, he had to convince Gloria. She was not sure it would be a good idea. She had just started

With the addition of Gloria, the Miami Latin Boys became the Miami Sound Machine.

college. Emilio explained that the band would only perform on weekends and during vacations.

Finally, with the encouragement of her grandmother, Gloria joined the group. So did her cousin Merci. Now that there were two young women in the band, they could not call themselves the Miami Latin Boys. This is how the Miami Sound Machine was born.

Although Gloria was excited about the band, she did not want to forget her studies. She worked to keep her grades up. After classes, Gloria would go to rehearsals. She had a lot of fun singing on weekends. She even found time to work as a translator at Miami International Airport. Things were working out better than she had expected.

Though Gloria was used to pop, the band still played mostly Latin music. Gloria had to become familiar with salsa and Latin rhythms. It brought her back to the days of her childhood. She remembered singing Cuban songs with the women in her Miami neighborhood. In time, Gloria was again at home with the Latin rhythms.

With Gloria and Merci singing, more music lovers became interested in the band. Since they had added pop songs and ballads to their performances, they attracted both Hispanic and non–Hispanic audiences. The band was developing their own special sound. Soon they were Miami's most popular local band.

Up to that point, the Miami Sound Machine was

The Miami Sound Machine soon developed their own special sound, making it a hit with both Hispanic and non-Hispanic audiences.

only playing material that other people had written and performed. Now it was time for the next step. They needed to create their own music. Gloria and a drummer in the band, Enrique "Kiki" Garcia, began writing songs and making up melodies.

All during this time, Emilio and Gloria were becoming more and more interested in each other. Finally, on July 4, 1976, they admitted their feelings and shared their first kiss. Working together had given them the opportunity to get to know one another as people, and respect each other as musicians. Now they began dating but decided to take things slowly.

In 1978, Gloria graduated from Miami University with a degree in psychology. After two years of dating, Emilio proposed to Gloria on February 12, 1978. He had meant to ask her on Valentine's Day, but he could not wait. They were married on September 1 of the same year. It was Gloria's twenty-first birthday. Emilio was now earning a good salary at the import firm. The couple were able to have their honeymoon in Japan.

Then it was back to work. The band recorded their first album, *Renacer*, for a small record company based in Miami. Translated into English, the title means "to be reborn." All the songs were a mixture of Spanish and English. The album sold well in their hometown. So did two other albums they recorded on their own label. The band was learning the ropes of the music business. They were getting ready for their big break.

The break came in 1980. It was an important year in the lives of Gloria and Emilio. First, there was a wonderful event. The Estefans had their first child, a boy they named Nayib. Then there was a tragic event. Gloria's father's battle with multiple sclerosis ended sadly with his death.

By then, Emilio had quit his job to spend all his time promoting the band. Soon they had a record contract with Discos CBS International, a division of CBS Records. It was a reason to celebrate. Still, there was one problem. The band could only record songs in Spanish. "They thought we would sell better in Latin America if we sang in Spanish," Gloria explains.

By 1983, the band had recorded four albums on their new label. Gloria's cousin Merci had left the

In the early 1980s, the Miami Sound Machine was playing to huge audiences all over Latin America.

band, so Gloria now did all the lead singing. Her voice was heard on the radio throughout Latin America. The Miami Sound Machine grew very popular in these countries. With each album, their number of fans grew by the thousands. The band played in large stadiums. Gloria and her band were superstars to the citizens of Panama, Venezuela, and Peru.

Back home in the United States, however, most people still had never heard of them. The band wanted to change that. Their chance came with an up-tempo tune called "Dr. Beat."

RHYTHM IS GONNA GET YOU

To reach a bigger audience in the U.S., the Miami Sound Machine needed to record in English. Finally, Emilio convinced CBS to let the band record one song in English. The band knew just which song to do. Kiki Garcia had composed "Dr. Beat" as a fun, upbeat disco piece. Everyone in the band loved it. Kiki wrote it in English first. Then he tried translating it into Spanish, but it just did not work.

The people at CBS decided to release "Dr. Beat" on the back, or "B," side of a Spanish **single**. Usually, "B" sides are not played on the radio. But the band got lucky. A Miami DJ was curious to hear the song with the English title. He played "Dr. Beat" on his Spanish-language station. Spanish and then English-language stations everywhere soon began playing the song. In England, the song even made it to number six on the Top Ten chart. The band flew there to perform their song on British television. "Dr. Beat" was an instant hit in Europe.

Hits like "Conga" and "Words Get in the Way" would launch Gloria Estefan on the road to superstardom in the United States.

The song was less of a hit in the U.S. Still, it was well-known in American dance clubs. That was enough for the CBS executives. They gave the group the go-ahead to record their next album in English! The result was an album called *Eyes of Innocence*, released in 1984.

In 1985, the Miami Sound Machine released a second English album, *Primitive Love.* It was the hit album the band had dreamed of. The funny thing was that the first smash single off that album was "Conga." The song was based on a traditional Cuban dance, also called the "conga." Some DJs were surprised. They had thought the song was too Latin-sounding, too "ethnic" for the tastes of U.S. listeners. In fact, the listeners went crazy for it!

What is most important to music lovers is a good song—and "Conga" was good. It was so good, in fact, that it hit the pop chart, the black chart, the dance chart, and the Latin chart all at the same time! "Conga" was the first single to manage that in the history of the Top Forty.

Other hits soon followed. The band's third single to make the charts, "Words Get in the Way," was very different from their first two hits. It was a ballad, Gloria's favorite type of song. She had written the **lyrics** and music herself. It made the Top Five and became the band's biggest hit so far. The Miami Sound Machine was on a roll!

In 1986, Gloria was asked to sing on two movie

The band's growing success was a source of pride in their hometown. The street where Gloria and Emilio lived was renamed Miami Sound Machine Boulevard.

soundtracks. Sylvester Stallone hired the Miami Sound Machine to write a song for his movie *Cobra*. They came up with the song titled "Suave." The word is Spanish for "smooth" or "soft." The next film was the hit *Top Gun*, starring Tom Cruise. On that soundtrack the band can be heard performing "Hot Summer Nights." By this time, the band had also begun making music videos.

With the band's rising popularity, U.S. fans were getting to know and love Gloria. She was the one who stood out in the music videos. Hers was the voice everyone heard. Gloria soon broke out as the star of the group. "I didn't want to be in the spotlight," she says. "But lead singers have to be out front, and people start recognizing you."

Soon, the Miami Sound Machine left for a world tour. Gloria and Emilio were saddened that they could not take their son along. A nine-month tour was too long for Nayib to be away from school. He stayed home in Miami with relatives.

During the tour, the band performed at the Tokyo Music Festival as representatives of the United States. They won the grand prize! When they returned home, the band was honored in another way. The street where Gloria and Emilio lived in Miami was renamed. It became Miami Sound Machine Boulevard. The street was not the only thing that got a new name. The band's next album was released in 1987 under the name "Gloria Estefan and the Miami Sound Machine."

The band's new record, *Let It Loose*, went platinum. In fact, the album actually sold over four million copies! Two dance tunes, "1-2-3" and "Rhythm Is Gonna Get You," were big hits. One of Gloria's beautiful ballads, "Anything for You," also made it all the way to number one in the United States.

The band's second big tour stretched to twenty months. That was more than twice as long as their last one. It was great for the band. They were becoming a huge success. Gloria and Emilio, however, had made a big decision. Emilio would stay home with Nayib, and also concentrate on being the band's producer. He would miss Gloria when she was away on tour, but this way, Nayib would have his father around. That was really important to both Emilio and Gloria.

The young couple was used to spending "twenty-four hours a day together," says Gloria. "So it was difficult to get used to." She adds, "It's been a growth process for both of us."

Gloria, Emilio, and the band began receiving many music awards. Billboard magazine gave the band 18 awards in their 1988 "The Year in Music" issue. At the 1989 American Music Awards, the band was named the Best Pop/Rock Group.

The Miami Sound Machine received the award for Best Pop/Rock Group at the American Music Awards in 1989.

In 1989, the band changed their name one last time. Now, they went solely under the name of their lead singer, Gloria Estefan. They released a new album called *Cuts Both Ways*. After disagreements with Emilio, Kiki Garcia had left the band. So seven out of the ten songs on the record were written by Gloria. One of them, called "Don't Wanna Lose You," went to number one on the charts. Gloria's songwriting talent started getting more attention.

Having built up such a great following, Gloria had to give more and more concerts. They sold out faster and faster. The band started off their newest tour in

On March 19, 1990, Emilio and Nayib joined Gloria at the White House, where she was honored by President George Bush.

Europe. When Gloria returned to the U.S. in 1989, she caught the flu. She could not stop coughing. All that coughing finally broke a blood vessel in her throat. The good news was that it would heal. The bad news was that she had to stop talking for two weeks. Even worse, she had to stop singing for two months! If she did not do this, she might ruin her voice forever. Gloria was scared. She could not imagine a life without singing. Emilio called off the band's upcoming tour until Gloria could get better.

By January 1990, Gloria was well again. That month, she performed at the American Music Awards and the Grammy Awards. Soon, Gloria also returned to concert touring.

In March, Gloria took time off from her tour to visit the White House. There she was honored by President George Bush for her work against drug abuse. Gloria had appeared in ads telling young people, "If you need someone, call a friend. Don't do drugs." From Washington, D.C., she headed for a concert date in Syracuse, New York. Unfortunately, tragedy struck on the Pennsylvania highway.

GET ON YOUR FEET

The accident happened on Tuesday, March 20, 1990. When rescue crews finally arrived, the scene was frightening. The front and back of Gloria Estefan's tour bus were smashed. Gloria herself was in great pain. Rescue workers laid her flat on a board and carried her out of the bus. Gloria remembers snowflakes hitting her face as she was hurried to the ambulance.

Gloria was sure her back was broken. Emilio refused to believe it was that serious. He did not want to think that his wife could be so badly hurt. When doctors examined Gloria, they told her that she was right. She would need an operation. Emilio fainted when he heard the news.

Gloria was not the only one who had been hurt in the accident. At first, Emilio thought he had only a cut on his hand. He was so worried about his wife and son, he did not realize until later that his shoulder had been separated, and he had also broken one of his ribs. Their son, Nayib, had broken his collarbone.

Gloria's injury, however, was certainly the worst. She was taken for surgery to the Hospital for Joint Diseases in New York City. Her operation took four hours. Dr. Michael Neuwirth fastened two steel rods to Gloria's spinal column. They were each eight inches long and had hooks that attached to the small bones in her spine. At the end of the operation, Gloria had four hundred stitches down her back.

The surgery had gone well, but there was still a chance that Gloria could become paralyzed. Gloria remembered how M.S. had disabled her father. The doctors, however, had hope for Gloria. Dr. Neuwirth said that if Gloria healed properly, she should be able

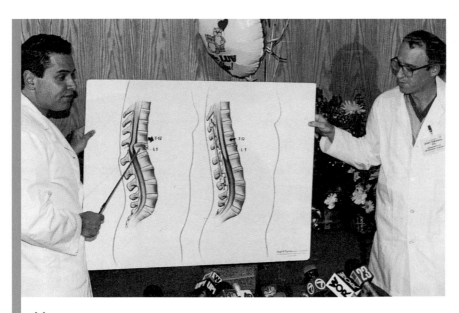

Millions of fans were worried about Gloria. Doctors at the Hospital for Joint Diseases describe her injuries and surgery for television audiences.

to do anything, "even dance." Emilio spoke to the press the day after the operation and said, "I don't care if she can't dance, just that she's alive."

No matter what, it would take at least three to six months of physical therapy and exercise for Gloria to feel back to normal. First, Gloria would have to wear a plastic brace and teach herself how to walk again.

Flowers, cards, telegrams, and letters arrived at the hospital by the thousands. Devoted fans sent Gloria encouraging messages. President George Bush called her twice. Wishes were also sent by performers such as Elton John, Jon Bon Jovi, Bruce Springsteen, Madonna, and Julio Iglesias, the world-famous Latin singer. Julio, a close friend of the Estefans, offered Gloria the use of his private jet. She could fly home on it when she was ready. Two weeks after her surgery, Gloria was ready.

The day Gloria was released from the hospital, photographers filled the hospital lobby. When they saw Gloria in her wheelchair, cameras began flashing everywhere. Gloria was tired, but she managed to smile for all the people who had shown up to support her. Someone asked her if she could stand, so Gloria got up and everyone clapped. Then she was wheeled away. At the airport, Julio Iglesias' jet was waiting to fly her to Miami. There, another crowd would warmly welcome her home.

The Estefans had bought a new house after they became music superstars. This house was on a tiny

With Emilio's help, Gloria stands up for the crowds as she leaves the hospital two weeks after surgery.

island named Star Island, still part of Miami but very private. Now the Estefans installed a gym. That way Gloria could work out at home. Gloria would have to exercise and lift weights for three hours, five times a week. She knew she would have to do this for the rest of her life.

Gloria stuck to it. The image of her father haunted her. "The most difficult thing of this injury was… what it would be like for my family," she said. Gloria did not want Emilio and Nayib to suffer the way she and her family had when caring for her father. She did everything she could to speed along her recovery. She was often in terrible pain, but she never complained.

Gloria was missing from the public eye, but her voice was not missing from the radio. CBS released a record of her greatest Spanish hits called *Exitos de Gloria Estefan*. "Exitos" is the Spanish word for "hits."

In the meantime, Gloria had a lot of time on her hands. She was thinking about her accident and about all the support she had received from her friends, family, and fans. She decided to write about these things. So Gloria began to compose songs again. Together they became the album *Into the Light*.

A year after the accident, Gloria and Emilio launched her *Into the Light* world tour. It started in her beloved Miami. Gloria's fans were thrilled. At her comeback concerts, audiences chanted, "Gloria! Gloria! Gloria!" They were excited to see their favorite star back in action. The day she left the hospital, Gloria had said, "I'll see you back on the road." Now she was keeping her word! Fans did not know how well she would be able to dance—or if she could dance at all. They did know it would be wonderful to see Gloria healthy and singing again.

The *Into the Light* concerts had a special opening. First, drums started beating. Then, singers began singing and chanting from behind a screen. Next,

Gloria announces her comeback concert tour at a press conference in Miami.

Gloria and the band during their 1991 comeback tour. Gloria was back—and better than ever!

dancers slipped onto the stage in glittering bodysuits and dark masks. They leaped and kicked all together. They wove back and forth, jumped, and swung flash-lights. It was as if they were searching for something. Then the drumming got faster and faster. The singers chanted louder. Excitement mounted. What was going to happen? Where was Gloria?

The smallest dancer was a woman. Suddenly, the other dancers lifted her up onto their shoulders. She tore off her mask. Down tumbled her long, brown curls. She grinned at the audience. The audience was shocked. Then they went wild. Gloria was back!

Gloria charged the audience up even more as she began to sing the fast, upbeat "Get on Your Feet." The song was just right. Gloria Estefan was back on *her* feet! The audience got up to clap, dance, and cheer.

After such a serious injury, it did not seem possible. Yet there was Gloria, dancing and singing better than ever! She said a lot of her recovery was thanks to the prayers and positive feelings her fans had been sending her. "It was like an energy I could feel in the hospital," she says. "It helped me to bear all the pain."

Gloria had a special custom at her concerts. At one point during the night, fans were allowed to line up and shake her hand as she sang. Some fans took turns presenting her with roses or stuffed animals. Others pressed personal notes into her hand. Many people were surprised that Gloria would allow her fans to get so close to her. But Gloria has always thought that her fans are very important. She even knows some of them by name. As for the fans, they knew that Gloria was worth waiting for—and they were right!

Chapter *Six*

LIVE FOR LOVING YOU

Gloria Estefan is not yet forty years old. Yet, by the time her comeback tour was over, she already had plenty of successes to look back on. It is not Gloria's style to sit back and remember her old achievements. She prefers to keep recording and trying new things. She loves her family, music, working, and living.

In 1993, Gloria released two solo albums. The first was called *Mi Tierra*. Translated from Spanish, the title means, "My Land." On this record, Gloria returned to her Cuban roots. Emilio and Gloria had made the record to show their love and loyalty to their heritage and their homeland. The album was made up of ballads. They were songs that spoke to the heart with beauty, and sometimes with sadness. The songs were all sung in Spanish, but they were also meant for English-speaking audiences.

The Estefans wondered how American listeners would react to *Mi Tierra*. It was not the typical pop

In 1993, Gloria Estefan's star was added to the Hollywood Walk of Fame on Hollywood Boulevard. Among the proud onlookers are Gloria's mother, standing behind her, and Emilio, in sunglasses.

music that Gloria's fans were used to. Although it did not sell as well as her usual pop albums, it still sold well. It also received strong reviews from critics. The singles could be heard on the radio on both Spanish and English stations.

For her Hispanic-American fans, Gloria was once again singing in the language of her culture and theirs. Cuban Americans were especially touched by the ballads. English–speaking audiences found Gloria's new sound to be refreshing and different. The words to her songs were translated into English on a lyric sheet, so everyone could understand what Gloria was singing about. With *Mi Tierra*, Gloria's dream of being a communicator and translator came true. Yet again, she broke language barriers with her music.

Gloria's next project was a Christmas album. It was called *Christmas Through Your Eyes*. The experience allowed Gloria to record her favorite Christmas carols and to share them with her listeners. That same year, Gloria was honored with a star on California's famous Hollywood "Walk of Fame."

In 1994, Gloria and Emilio found out they were going to have another baby. The doctors told them that the baby would be a girl. The Estefans decided to call her Emily, after her father, Emilio. While Gloria was still pregnant, she would sing to little Emily. "She's got very distinctive tastes," Gloria said about her child. "There are songs she's reacting to, she's hearing it full blast because my voice is coming straight down to her." Perhaps little Emily will grow up to be in the music business like her parents. Nayib has already mentioned his interest in following in his mother's footsteps. He wants to be a singer.

While waiting for the new baby to be born, Gloria kept busy. She released yet another album. *Hold Me, Thrill Me, Kiss Me* was a record of **cover** songs. A "cover" is a song that has already been sung by someone else. Gloria chose several favorites she had heard when she was growing up. She gave them a

The Estefans' Miami restaurants celebrate Hispanic cultures. Here, Gloria walks outside the Cardozo Hotel, which she and Emilio own.

flavor that was all her own. For fans, the album was like having two old friends—the familiar songs and Gloria herself—get together. The result was magic. Gloria's single "Turn the Beat Around" was a cover of a disco song from the 1970s. The song made the Top Forty pop charts immediately after it was released.

Gloria and Emilio had decided they wanted to do something for the Cuban community in Miami, to pay them back for all their support. The Estefans bought a building in South Beach, which is very close to their island home. There they opened up a restaurant called Lario's on the Beach. Their goal was to have an all-Cuban restaurant. They wanted patrons to hear live Cuban music, see Cuban decorations, taste Cuban dishes, and be surrounded by Spanish-speaking people. They wanted a restaurant that made people feel like they were in Cuba. The idea worked. Lario's on the Beach is now one of the hottest eating spots in South Beach.

Next, Emilio and Gloria bought the Cardozo Hotel. They opened a second restaurant in the lobby. The specialty there is food from Spain. The hotel became another great success for the Estefans.

On December 5, 1994, Gloria and Emilio gave something else to Miami. Their daughter, Emily Marie Estefan, was born. Dr. Nidia Iglesias, who helped to deliver the baby, told the press that Gloria and Emily were fine. However, Emilio had become over-excited and very nervous. "We had to help him out for a few seconds there because he almost fainted," the doctor told reporters.

Things have never been better for Gloria. She has recovered from her accident. Her career is still going strong. She has also played a large role in giving Hispanic cultures some of the exposure they deserve. Through her songs, Gloria has brought the acceptance of Hispanic rhythms and styles to popular music. With her restaurants, Gloria is helping to spread Hispanic cultures through the food and atmosphere they offer. By recording and speaking in both English and Spanish, she has managed to communicate with people all over the world. Yet, even with these accomplishments, Gloria believes that true happiness is found somewhere else.

At the 1994 Grammy Awards, Gloria won an award for her album of ballads in Spanish, a tribute to her Cuban roots.

One of Gloria's favorite songs is one she and Emilio co-wrote with Diane Warren for the *Into the Light* album. It is called "Live for Loving You." The words ring true for Gloria. Real success is to love and be loved by your family. Today, Gloria Estefan can look at her life with her husband and her children, and know that she has made it.

Important Dates

1957   Born in Havana, Cuba, on September 1.

1959   Moves to the United States with her family.

1974   Joins Emilio Estefan's band, which is renamed the Miami Sound Machine.

1976   *Renacer*, the band's first album, is released.

1978   Marries Emilio Estefan. Receives a bachelor's degree in psychology from Miami University.

1980   First child, a son named Nayib, is born.

1981   The band begins recording albums in Spanish for CBS.

1984   "Dr. Beat," the band's first English-language single, becomes a hit. Records *Eyes of Innocence*.

1985   The Miami Sound Machine releases *Primitive Love*.

1987   *Let It Loose* is released.

1989   *Cuts Both Ways* comes out. The band changes its name to "Gloria Estefan."

1990   Suffers injury in a bus accident. *Exitos de Gloria Estefan* is released.

1991   Makes her comeback. *Into the Light* is released.

1993   *Mi Tierra*, *Christmas Through Your Eyes*, and *Greatest Hits* albums are released.

1994   *Hold Me, Thrill Me, Kiss Me* is released. Second child, a daughter named Emily, is born.

Glossary

ballads   Slow songs about tender feelings, usually romantic or sad.

bilingual   Having the ability to communicate in two languages.

cover   A remake or re-recording of a song that was originally recorded by another artist.

lyrics   The words of a song.

single   One song from a new album, released by itself, usually on a cassette with two sides, "A" and "B."

Bibliography

Catalano, Grace. *Gloria Estefan*. New York: St. Martin's, 1991.

Gernand, Renée. *The Cuban Americans*. New York: Chelsea House, 1991.

Harrington, Richard. "Hot: Gloria Estefan Powers the Miami Sound Machine." *New York Newsday*, July 23, 1988.

Shirley, David. *Gloria Estefan*. New York: Chelsea House, 1994.

Index

ANDERSON ELEMENTARY SCHOOL

105140152   782.42164 ROD

Gloria Estefan

782.
42164   Rodriguez, Janel.
ROD   Gloria Estefan

DATE DUE	BORROWER'S NAME	ROOM NUMBER

782.
42164   Rodriguez, Janel.
ROD   Gloria Estefan